TAXI
This book belongs to:
Name ....
Date ....

ACKNOWLEDGEMENTS

Commissioned and project managed by Duck Egg Blue Limited

Author: Kait Eaton
Editor: Kate Baker
Illustrator: Daniel Rieley
Design: Duck Egg Blue Limited
Publishing Director: Piers Pickard
Publisher: Rebecca Hunt
Editorial Director: Joe Fullman
Art Director: Andy Mansfield
Print Production: Nigel Longuet

Published in October 2023 by
Lonely Planet Global Limited
CRN: 554153
ISBN: 978 1 83758 104 7
www.lonelyplanet.com/kids

10 9 8 7 6 5 4 3 2

Printed in China

Credits
The publisher would like to thank the following for their kind permission to reproduce their images in this book:

Shutterstock.com: darsi, ideyweb, Natthareya, TALVA

MIX
Paper | Supporting responsible forestry
FSC™ C021741
www.fsc.org

Paper in this book is certified against the Forest Stewardship Council™ standards. FSC™ promotes environmentally responsible, socially beneficial and economically viable management of the world's forests.

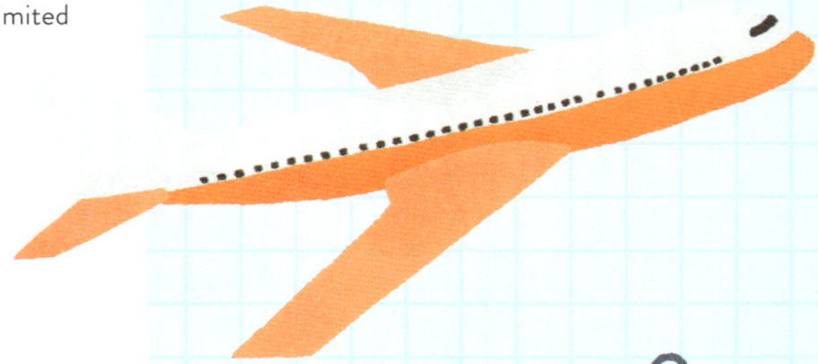

STAY IN TOUCH

lonelyplanet.com/contact

Lonely Planet Offices:
IRELAND
Digital Depot, Roe Lane
(off Thomas St), Digital Hub,
Dublin 8, D08 TCV4, Ireland

UNITED KINGDOM
The Cooperage, 5 Copper Row,
London SE1 2LH, United Kingdom

lonely planet KIDS

Create Your Own Travel Journal

WRITTEN BY KAIT EATON
ILLUSTRATED BY DANIEL RIELEY

USING YOUR TRAVEL JOURNAL

Holidays are all about exciting adventures, new discoveries and **making lots of memories**.

No matter how far you're travelling, or how you plan to get there, this book will help you record all your amazing experiences and provide the perfect keepsake to treasure for years to come.

Each chapter will help you document a different part of your trip:

CHAPTER 1 > BEFORE THE OFF

Fill in your plans, hopes and dreams ahead of the big day.

CHAPTER 2 > GETTING THERE

Record the journey and keep entertained with a variety of boredom busters.

CHAPTER 3 > YOU'VE ARRIVED!

This chapter is all about the holiday itself. Write, draw or stick in items to help remember special memories as you make them.

CHAPTER 4 > MEMORIES TO CHERISH

Make a note of all the best bits, recognise special achievements and start planning your next trip!

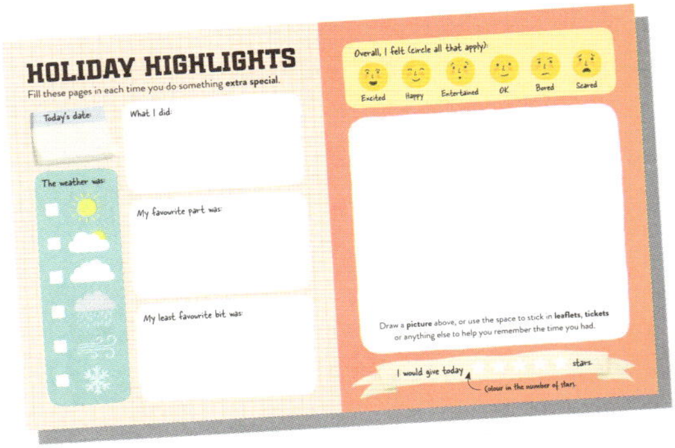

Document your **HOLIDAY HIGHLIGHTS** on pages 54–63.

Use the pages at the back of the book for extra scribbling space, or to stick in tickets, postcards, photos and more.

CONTENTS

Use this space to sketch your **three dream holiday destinations.**

Dream destination #1

Dream destination #2

Dream destination #3

BEFORE THE OFF

"It's a **big world** out there. It would be a shame not to experience it."

– **J. D. Andrews**

MY HOLIDAY

What do you know about your **travel plans**?

I am going to...

I am going with...

We are travelling by...

I hope the weather is...

I will be gone for

days.

I feel...

What do you think will be **different** about where you're going from where you live?

DESTINATION FACT FILE

Do some **research** on where you're going on holiday and see if you can find out the following information:

Holiday destination: ....

Continent: ....

Country or state: ....

Capital city: ....

Main language(s) spoken: ....

Currency: .... **Population:** ....

Native creatures: ....

Climate: ....

What kinds of things is the place you are going to **famous for**? Draw them here.

WHERE IN THE WORLD?

Can you **draw a map** of where you are going?

Label other countries and cities if you can.
Don't forget to include seas, lakes and rivers.
What does the flag look like? Sketch it below.

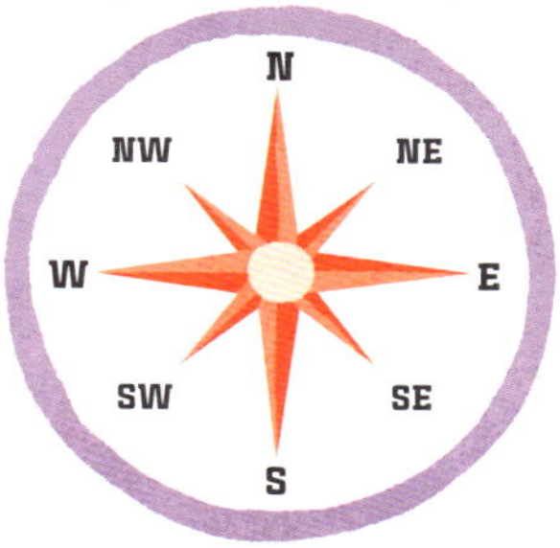

HOWDY!

Do they speak a **different language** where you're going? Make a note of some **important phrases** you might need.

Hello! How are you?

Write the phrase in English and the translation below.

If English is the main language where you're going, make a note of some popular sayings you might hear instead.

THINGS TO DO

Draw what there will be to **see, do and experience** on your holiday.

What are you **most excited** about doing?

Is there anything you really **DON'T** want to do?

TASTE BUD TINGLERS

What **types of food** might you try on holiday? Fill in the menus with **typical dishes** from your destination.

MENU

Starter

Main Course

Dessert

MENU

Starter

Main Course

Dessert

Which do you like the sound of, and which might you avoid?

Use this space to draw what food you are most looking forward to trying.

I'd like to try the dish above,

but I think I'll give .... a miss!

TRAVEL BUDDIES

Who is going **on holiday** with you?
Draw their pictures here.

I will miss this person while I'm away...

Choose someone you're going on holiday with. What do you think they are **looking forward to** the most? Ask them to fill in this page. Were you right?

My name is:

I am most excited about:

I feel like this when I think about our holiday:

Ask them to draw a face to show how they feel.

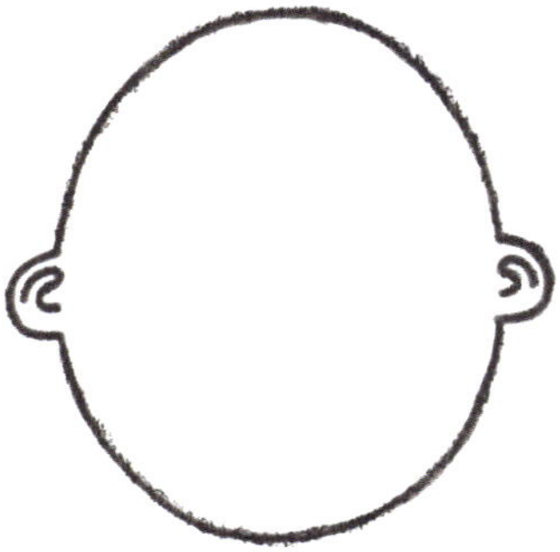

TRAVELLING ABOUT

There are **so many different ways** to get from place to place. What transport do you think you might take on your trip?

Train ☐

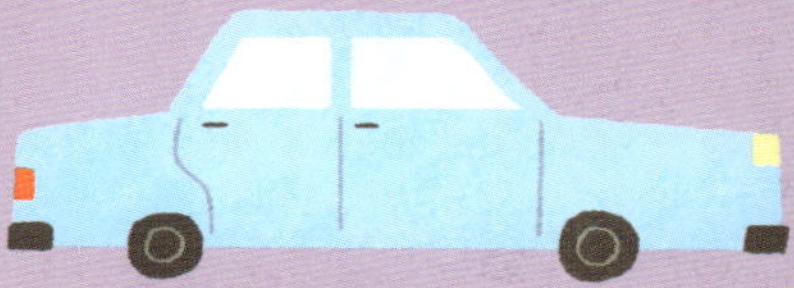

Car ☐

Taxi ☐

Bus ☐

Circle the ones you think you'll use, then tick them off while you're on holiday to see which you got right.

Hot air balloon ☐

Coach ☐

Aeroplane ☐

Think about how you will travel for the journey and how you might get around while you're there.

Helicopter ☐

Underground train ☐

Scooter ☐

Bicycle ☐

Ferry / Cruise ship ☐

Campervan ☐

Hovercraft ☐

Any others?

WHAT TO PACK?

Toothpaste? Check. Underwear? Check. Travel journal? Check! Draw pictures of **the things you plan to take with you**, then **tick them off** as you pack.

Toothpaste

Comfy shoes

What could you not possibly live without? Sketch **some of your favourite things** that you **absolutely must** take on your trip.

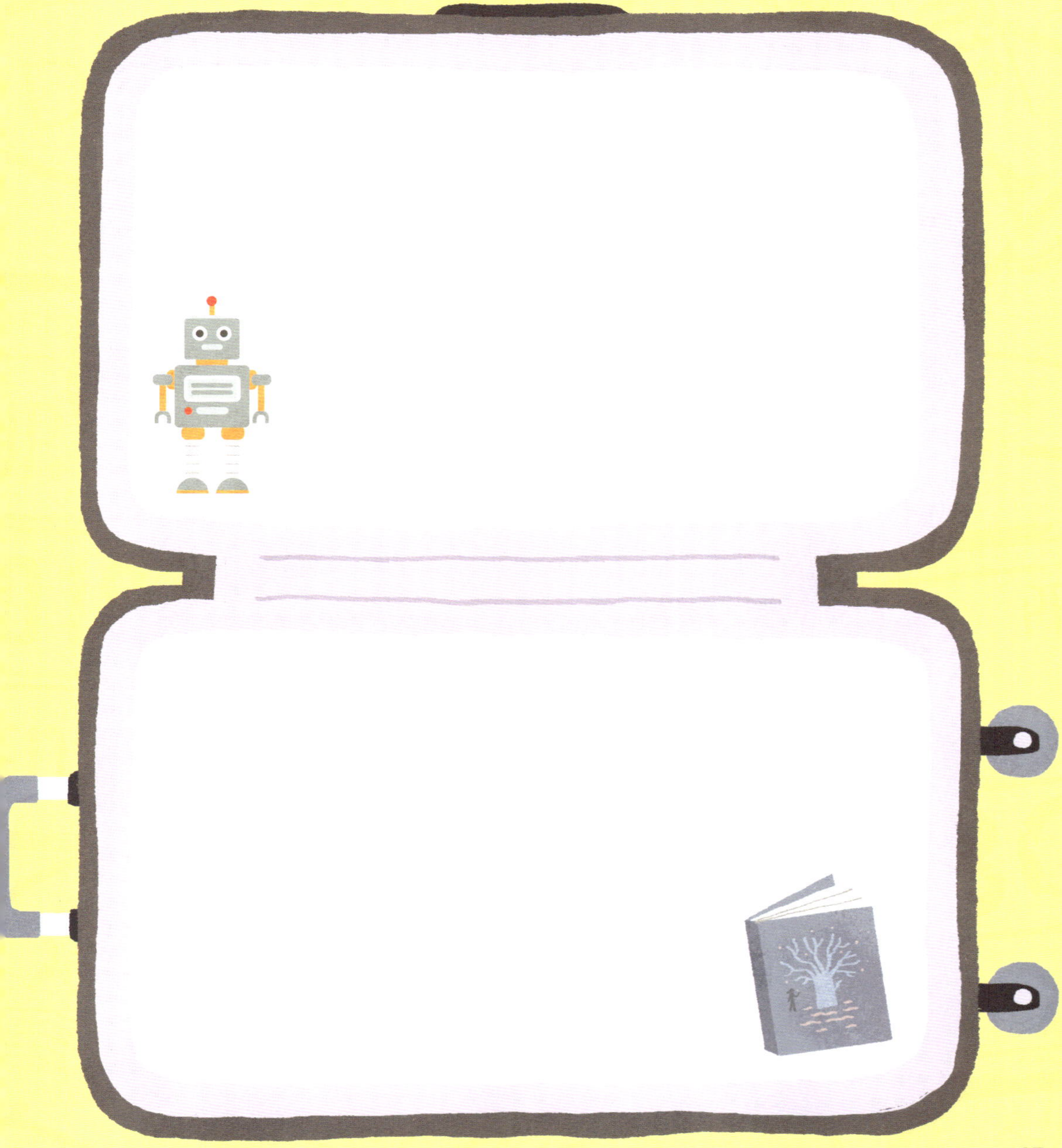

Use this space to sketch **three funny things** you see while you're travelling.

Funny thing #1

Funny thing #2

Funny thing #3

GETTING THERE

"The gladdest moment in human life is a departure into **unknown lands.**"

– Richard Burton

YOU'RE OFF!

Today's the **big day**. How are you feeling about the journey? Are you excited? Nervous? Scared?

Draw your emotions or mood here.

Complete the details on your passport.

NAME

AGE

HEIGHT

HAIR COLOUR

EYE COLOUR

Draw your picture here.

DISTINGUISHING FEATURES

PLACES ALREADY VISITED

Fill this area with passport stamps to show other places you've been, or list them.

TRAVEL PLANS

What **important information** do you know about your journey? Use the spaces below to fill in as many details as you can.

We need to leave home at:

We hope to arrive at:

The journey should take this long:

What else do you know about how you're getting there?

Will you stop on the way?

PICK YOUR PLAYLIST

I will be listening to:

1 ....
2 ....
3 ....
4 ....
5 ....
6 ....
7 ....
8 ....
9 ....
10 ....
11 ....
12 ....

Every journey needs a selection of carefully chosen **feel-good tunes**. Make a note of your favourite tracks and compose your very own travel playlist.

What do the people you're travelling with like to listen to?

LOTS OF LUGGAGE

Draw what **all your luggage** looks like, and label whose is whose.

Become a **luggage designer**. Use coloured pens or pencils to decorate this suitcase with a **striking, eye-catching** design.

WHO DO YOU SEE?

Sketch the **faces of people** you spot on your journey.

LOOKING OUT

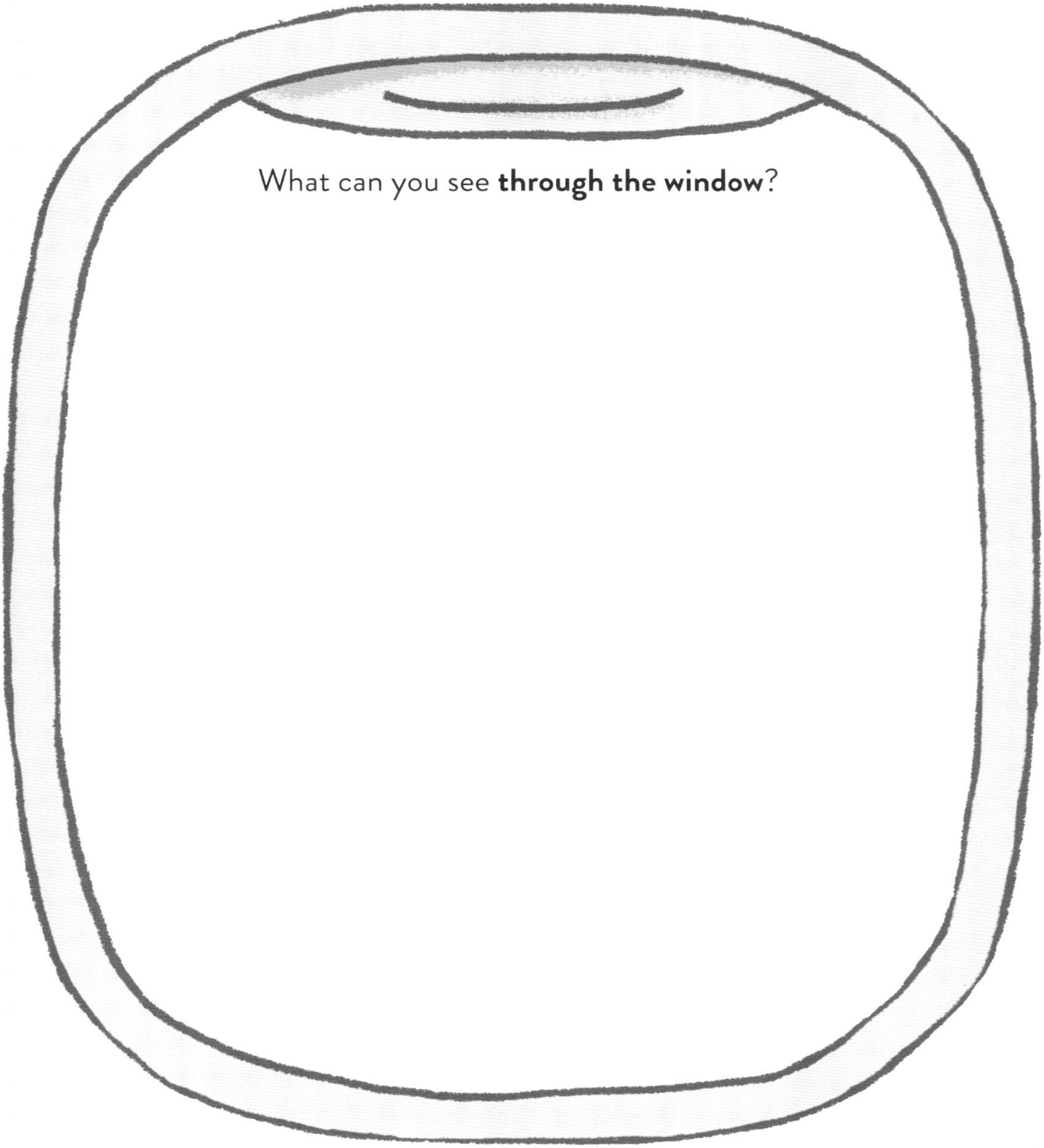

What can you see **through the window**?

MUNCHIES ON THE MOVE

Draw the snacks you've **packed for your trip** in the lunchbox.

CHIT CHAT

What have you and your buddies been **talking about?** Have you overheard any **funny conversations** from other travellers? Make a note of them below.

WHAT CAN YOU SPOT?

Travelling often involves a lot of **waiting around** and down time. Keep **boredom at bay** by ticking off these items as you see them.

☐ **A traffic cone**

☐ **Someone drinking a hot drink**

☐ **Someone wearing sunglasses**

☐ **A red bag**

☐ **Someone taking a selfie**

☐ **An umbrella**

An empty coach

Someone walking two dogs

Something blowing in the wind

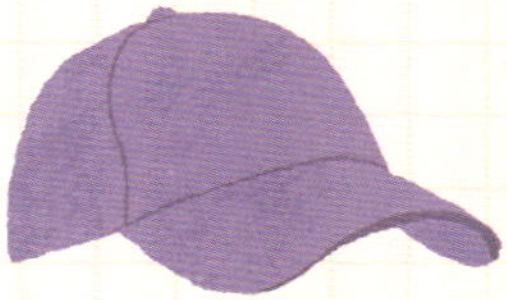

Someone wearing a cap

Someone playing a game

Something blue

Something broken

A crying baby

Something sparkly

HOW'S YOUR MEMORY?

You might be doing a lot of sitting around, but you can still give your **brain cells a workout**! Look at this page for 30 seconds, then turn to page 46 and see if you can **answer the questions**.

SO MANY SQUARES

You'll need at least one other player for this **simple-but-addictive game**.

Grab a pen each and take it in turns to draw a horizontal or vertical line between two adjacent dots. If your line completes a square, claim it by writing your initial in the middle of it. Take an extra turn each time you complete a square. The winner is the player who has claimed the most squares at the end of the game!

Once you've completed this grid, you can use the pages at the end of the book to create another.

BOREDOM BUSTER #4

CHILL OUT AND COLOUR

Work on colouring a part of this pattern whenever you get a **quiet moment**, either while travelling or during your holiday.

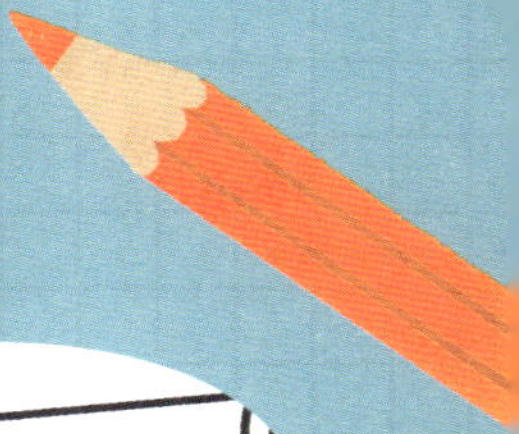

BOREDOM BUSTER #5

MUDDLE MOUTH

Try and **twist your tongue** around these **silly sentences.** Can you make up any of your own?

Red lorry, yellow lorry. (Repeat as many times as you can.)

I saw a kitten eating chicken in the kitchen.

Thin sticks, thick bricks. (Repeat as many times as you can.)

To begin to toboggan, first buy a toboggan, but don't buy too big a toboggan.

Surely she shall see the sun shine soon.

HOW'S YOUR MEMORY?

What can you **remember** from page 42?

- How many items are there altogether?
- What two items from nature are there?
- What is the time on the watch?
- Which musical instrument is shown?

CREATE YOUR OWN WORDSEARCH

Challenge a travel pal to find all the **hidden words**.

Think of ten words that are relevant to your trip. Write them in the space below, then copy them into the grid in any direction. Once all ten words are in place, fill the remaining squares with random letters and hand this book to someone you are travelling with to see if they can find them all.

1 ....

2 ....

3 ....

4 ....

5 ....

6 ....

7 ....

8 ....

9 ....

10 ....

You'll find pages with grids like this at the back of this book if you'd like to create another.

Use this space to sketch **three places you hope to visit.**

Place #1

Place #2

Place #3

YOU'VE ARRIVED!

"All we have to decide is **what to do** with the time that is given us."

– J.R.R. Tolkien

FIRST IMPRESSIONS

JOURNEY RECAP

We arrived at .... , which was earlier/later than expected.

Fill in the details about the place **you'll call home** while you're on holiday:

Accommodation name: ....

Room/lodge/pitch number: ....

How to get from the entrance or reception: ....

....

....

Name of the person who showed you around:

....

First impressions: ....

....

....

....

Sketch what your accommodation looks like **from the outside**.

Now draw what you can see **from the window**.

I would give this place ☆☆☆☆☆ stars.

Colour in the number of stars.

WHERE AM I?

Draw a map of where you are staying. First, sketch your accommodation, then add other details around it. Create a key to help other people understand what's what.

KEY

Water

Road

What is there to do in the area?
Make a list or draw pictures of **everything that sounds good**.

And the best thing is...

What do you want to do **first**?

What do you **not want to do**?

HOLIDAY HIGHLIGHTS

Fill these pages in each time you do something **extra special**.

Today's date:

The weather was:

What I did:

My favourite part was:

My least favourite bit was:

Overall, I felt (circle all that apply):

Excited Happy Entertained OK Bored Scared

Draw a **picture** above, or use the space to stick in **leaflets**, **tickets** or anything else to help you remember the time you had.

I would give today stars.

Colour in the number of stars.

HOLIDAY HIGHLIGHTS

Fill these pages in each time you do something **extra special**.

Today's date:

What I did:

The weather was:

My favourite part was:

My least favourite bit was:

Overall, I felt (circle all that apply):

Excited Happy Entertained OK Bored Scared

Draw a **picture** above, or use the space to stick in **leaflets**, **tickets** or anything else to help you remember the time you had.

I would give today stars.

Colour in the number of stars.

HOLIDAY HIGHLIGHTS

Fill these pages in each time you do something **extra special**.

Today's date:

What I did:

The weather was:

My favourite part was:

My least favourite bit was:

Overall, I felt (circle all that apply):

Excited Happy Entertained OK Bored Scared

Draw a **picture** above, or use the space to stick in **leaflets**, **tickets** or anything else to help you remember the time you had.

I would give today stars.

Colour in the number of stars.

HOLIDAY HIGHLIGHTS

Fill these pages in each time you do something **extra special**.

Today's date:

The weather was:

What I did:

My favourite part was:

My least favourite bit was:

Overall, I felt (circle all that apply):

Excited Happy Entertained OK Bored Scared

Draw a **picture** above, or use the space to stick in **leaflets**, **tickets** or anything else to help you remember the time you had.

I would give today stars.

Colour in the number of stars.

HOLIDAY HIGHLIGHTS

Fill these pages in each time you do something **extra special**.

Today's date:

The weather was:

What I did:

My favourite part was:

My least favourite bit was:

Overall, I felt (circle all that apply):

Excited | Happy | Entertained | OK | Bored | Scared

Draw a **picture** above, or use the space to stick in **leaflets**, **tickets** or anything else to help you remember the time you had.

I would give today stars.

Colour in the number of stars.

FANTASTIC FACTS

Holidays are all about **new discoveries.** Jot down any amazing info you've learned about the places you've visited or the things you've done.

I have learned all this awesome stuff:

SPECIAL SITES

What **special places or landmarks** have you been lucky enough to visit on your trip? Draw them or stick in pictures here.

Location and date:

Location and date:

Location and date:

Location and date:

SO FAR I'VE...

☐ **Eaten an ice cream**
Date: ....

☐ **Spoken a different language**
Date: ....

☐ **Tried a new food**
Date: ....

☐ **Made a new friend**
Date: ....

☐ **Entered a competition**
Date: ....

☐ **Gone to bed late**
Date: ....

☐ **Spent some holiday money**
Date: ....

Waited in a massive queue

Date: ....

Taken an awesome photo

Date: ....

Done something I've never done before

Date: ....

Laughed uncontrollably

Date: ....

Learned something new

Date: ....

Helped a stranger

Date: ....

Walked until my legs ached

Date: ....

Messaged someone at home

Date: ....

WHO DOES WHAT?

You'll meet many people doing **different jobs** on holiday, such as waiting staff, tour guides and hotel workers.

STAY SAFE

Make sure to only speak to other people when you have a grown-up with you.

Name:

Job:

Name:

Job:

Name:

Job:

The person I'll remember most is:

I won't forget them because:

NEW FLAVOURS

Be brave and eat something you've **never tried before**. What did it look like before you tucked in?

How was it? Would you eat it again?

☐ Awesome! ☐ Quite nice ☐ Hmm, so so ☐ Not great ☐ Disgusting!

MESSAGES HOME

Stuck for what to say on postcards to pals? When you have a **funny idea**, jot it down here for later use!

MAKING FRIENDS

Who are you **hanging out with** on holiday? Fill in the details of **new pals** here so you don't forget them when you go home.

Draw their picture here.

1

Name: ....

Age: ....

From: ....

Interesting fact: ....

....

2

Name: ....

Age: ....

From: ....

Interesting fact: ....

....

Choose one friend and fill in more details about them on page 74.

3

Name: ....

Age: ....

From: ....

Interesting fact: ....

....

4

Name: ....

Age: ....

From: ....

Interesting fact: ....

....

5

Name: ....

Age: ....

From: ....

Interesting fact: ....

....

6

Name: ....

Age: ....

From: ....

Interesting fact: ....

....

BEST BUDDIES

Choose one of your **new friends** to quiz and find out **all sorts of information** about them.

Name (and/or nickname): ....

From: ....

Brothers / sisters: ....

Pets: ....

Hobbies: ....

Favourite foods: ....

Where we first met: ....

Things we have in common: ....

....

....

....

....

....

NEW ADVENTURES

What have you **enjoyed doing on this holiday** that you've never done before?

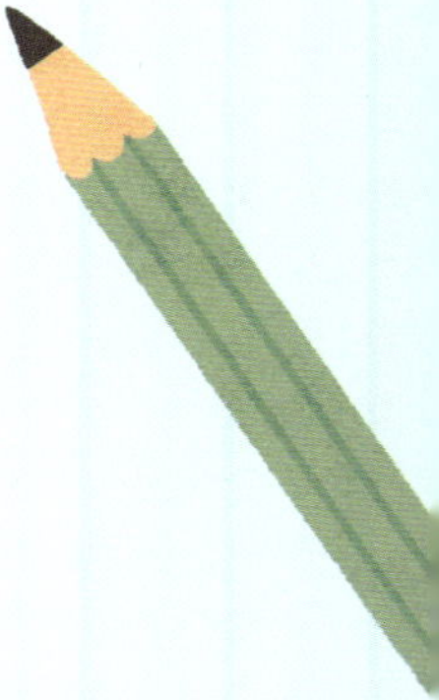

Is there anything you've done on this holiday that you **never, ever want to do again**? Why?

Use this space to sketch **three awesome things** you have done on your trip.

Awesome thing #1

Awesome thing #2

Awesome thing #3

MEMORIES TO CHERISH

"Things end, but
memories last forever."

– Kumar Milan

HOLIDAY HIGHLIGHTS

What were the **best bits** of your holiday? Fill them in here.

Most fun experience:

Tastiest meal:

Something I had never seen before on a menu:

Funniest thing I saw:

Best evening:

Earliest morning:

Best place I visited:

Most interesting fact I learned:

Most relaxing day:

Most exhausting thing I did:

Kindest stranger:

Best thing I bought:

Something I am grateful happened:

AWARDS AND ACCOLADES

It's time to recognise the **special achievements** of your travel companions. Who will **come out on top**?

Most adventurous eater:

Most stylish swimsuit:

Most likely to keep everyone waiting:

Longest lie-in:

Bravest explorer:

Most embarrassing:

Most forgetful:

Pickiest eater:

And the person with the most awards is...

All-round nice person:

SUPER SOUVENIRS

What souvenirs did you spot when **shopping on holiday**? Draw your favourites here.

Design a **souvenir t-shirt** to sum up your trip. It could show a place you visited or an awesome thing you did.

TIME TO GO

How does thinking about going home make you feel?

Would you like to come here again, or not? Why?

If you visited again, would you do anything different?

All **good things** must come to an end. Fill in the pages below, then look back to the start of the book to see if your holiday was **what you expected** it to be.

Is there anything you wished you had done or tried on holiday?

Can you think of anyone you know who might like to visit this place? What do you think they would enjoy most?

If you made a movie or wrote a book about your holiday, what would it be called?

HEADING HOME

Who are you **looking forward to seeing** most when you get home? Draw a picture of **you and them together**.

When I get home, one of the first things I want to do is:

....

INTO THE FUTURE...

Now you can start thinking about your **next trip**!
Where might you go?

Use this space for **lists**, **sketches** and **memories**, or if you need extra space for any of the activities in this book.

You could also use these pages to stick in photos and postcards!

Use this space for **lists, sketches** and **memories**, or if you need extra space for any of the activities in this book.

SYD
SYDNEY
AUSTRALIA
Weight:
Date:
Flight:

Use this space for **lists**, **sketches** and **memories**, or if you need extra space for any of the activities in this book.

50